WS

Please return/renew this item by the last date shown

worcestershire
countycouncil
Libraries & Learning

Author:
Fiona Macdonald studied history at Cambridge University, England, and at the University of East Anglia. She has taught in schools, adult education and universities, and is the author of numerous books for children on historical topics.

Artist:
David Antram was born in Brighton, England, in 1958. He studied at Eastbourne College of Art and then worked in advertising for fifteen years before becoming a full-time artist. He has illustrated many children's non-fiction books.

Series creator:
David Salariya was born in Dundee, Scotland. He has illustrated a wide range of books and has created and designed many new series for publishers in the UK and overseas. In 1989 he established The Salariya Book Company. He lives in Brighton with his wife, illustrator Shirley Willis, and their son Jonathan.

Editor: **Tanya Kant**

Editorial Assistant: **Mark Williams**

Published in Great Britain in 2009 by
Book House, an imprint of
The Salariya Book Company Ltd
25 Marlborough Place, Brighton BN1 1UB
www.salariya.com
www.book-house.co.uk

HB ISBN-13: 978-1-906714-15-4
PB ISBN-13: 978-1-906714-16-1

SALARIYA

1 3 5 7 9 8 6 4 2

A CIP catalogue record for this book is available from the British Library.

Printed and bound in China.
Printed on paper from sustainable sources.

Avoid being a Samurai!

Written by
Fiona Macdonald

Illustrated by
David Antram

Created and designed by
David Salariya

The Danger Zone

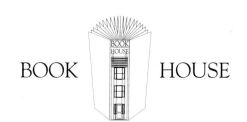

BOOK HOUSE

Contents

Introduction

Well, here we are! The place? Japan. The time? The early 17th century. And you – you're a young boy from an ordinary Japanese family. Like other boys, you've seen awesome *samurai* warriors marching off to war. And you've heard wonderful stories about samurai heroes who have won brave battles, performed amazing feats of swordsmanship, survived countless adventures – and have even had magical powers!

When you grow up, you'd like to be a samurai and astonish everyone with your courage and skill. But samurai life is hard and dangerous, as well as glamorous and exciting. For centuries, samurai have been fighting amongst themselves for wealth and power. There are new laws that aim to stop samurai wars, but these laws also prevent ordinary boys like you from becoming warriors. Perhaps that's not so bad! Read this book, think carefully, then ask yourself: 'Would I really want to be a samurai?'

Japanese society

JAPAN is an ancient, traditional society. Everyone knows their place and must show respect to their superiors. It is extremely difficult to move up social ranks.

Emperor and royal family

Shogun (top army commander)

Daimyo (ancient noble lords): they own estates and castles, and some lead armies.

Warlords: they lead armies and have won power by fighting.

Samurai and ashigaru (ordinary soldiers)

Farmers and their families

Not for you!

Samurai first became famous around AD 1200. At that time, any brave fighting man could apply to join a warlord's army as a samurai ('man who serves'). But in 1590, General Toyotomi Hideyoshi took control of Japan. He banned everyone except the samurai of that time – and their sons – from owning swords or fighting with them. You're just too late! Nowadays, samurai can be recruited only from old samurai families, not from ordinary families like yours.

Who can't be a samurai?

FARMERS are needed at home. They grow the food that keeps all Japanese people alive.

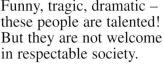

ENTERTAINERS. Funny, tragic, dramatic – these people are talented! But they are not welcome in respectable society.

Merchants, craftworkers and townspeople

Buddhist holy teachers, monks and nuns. Their rank depends on their family.

Don't be sad! You're not alone. Most people in Japan cannot be samurai, however much they admire samurai courage, dedication and skills. Samurai are elite, expert warriors. They share a proud history of war service, stretching back hundreds of years.

WOMEN AND GIRLS. Traditionally, Japanese people think that fighting is a task for men. There have been a few women warriors, but they are rare exceptions!

JAPAN IS WARY of foreigners. In the late 1200s, Mongol warriors from the Asian mainland tried to invade Japan. Recently, new strangers have arrived – Christian missionaries from Europe.

Handy hint

Unfortunately, you can't fight if you're left-handed! You might get in the way of your comrades who hold their swords in their right hands.

THE EMPEROR is the most honoured man in Japan, but the shogun is the most powerful. Since 1192, shoguns have ruled Japan on behalf of the emperors. *Shogun* means 'great general'.

Emperor

Samurai

Shogun

Tough training

SCHOOL will train a pupil's mind. Samurai families admire scholarship and knowledge.

Training to be a samurai begins when pupils are very young – at around seven years old! And it's very tough indeed. It aims to turn the most timid youngsters into powerful fighters, by teaching them all sorts of battle techniques and survival skills. As a student, you'd spend years learning how to handle weapons. You'd also study reading, history, poetry and handwriting.

Your training would also shape your character: a samurai must have good manners, obedience, respect for others and self-discipline. And you'd be taught to live – or die – for your comrades, as a loyal member of a team. Could you spend your childhood training this way? Or would you rather live peacefully at home with your friends and family?

BE BRAVE! Battle practice can be terrifying – and very painful. But pupils soon learn to defend themselves and fight back.

The pen and the sword in accord.*

But when do I get to fight?

READING AND WRITING are useful skills. They are also signs of a noble, gracious person.

On second thoughts, I think I'll be a farmer!

*Old Japanese phrase. It means 'Learning and fighting are equally important'.

PUPILS are taught to honour their teachers and fighting masters. These teachers are very wise – and worth listening to.

STUDY STRATEGY by playing traditional board games such as *go*. These will help a pupil to think ahead and outwit his enemies.

Handy hint

Be lucky! If you have bad luck, or have not studied hard, you might die in your first battle.

Great to graduate

AT AROUND 14 years old, pupils take part in a *genbuku* coming-of-age ceremony, and will be allowed to tie up their hair in special samurai style. Now they are ready to fight!

PUPILS LISTEN to stories about famous samurai who lived long ago. Their glorious adventures inspire everyone!

A special sword

Samurai fight with several different weapons: spears for stabbing and slashing, bows that shoot deadly arrows, and newly invented guns that fire metal balls. But a samurai's most important weapon – and his most treasured possession – is his long, sharp sword. The best swords have such fine, flexible blades that some people say they are alive!

Samurai like to have as many swords as possible. They can buy them (though swords are very expensive), inherit them from their fathers, capture them from dead enemies, or receive them as rewards for bravery. Wearing a sword is a sign of wealth, skill and high rank. So if you see a swordsman, be respectful.

SWORD FIGHTING. It takes a lifetime of learning to perfect fighting with a samurai sword. First, bow to your teacher, fighting partner – or enemy!

A samurai always sleeps with his sword by his side.*

THE BEST SWORDS are made by expert craftsmen, who can hammer, twist and fold iron into secret patterns. There are several sword designs. In battle, katana (shown right) are worn with the sharp edge uppermost.

Sharp edge

An old Japanese saying

THEN, draw your sword. Now you must try to do two things at once – attack your opponent and guard yourself against his attack.

IT'S NOT EASY! One of you will have to get your sword close enough to strike a winning blow. Will you be victorious?

Handy hint

Mind your fingers! Fit a *tsuba* (circular guard) to your sword-blade, to avoid accidentally cutting your hand.

Tsuba

That looks sharp!

Katana

Magic weapons

TALL TAIL? There are many amazing stories about samurai warriors and their swords. Famous, fearless Prince Yamato, who lived around 110 BC, was said to fight with a sword that was found in a magic serpent's tail!

11

Awkward armour

o you know how samurai survive a battle? You need skilful swordsmanship, bravery and luck. But, just as important, you need armour! Samurai protect their heads with helmets and their bodies with elaborate suits of metal. Their chests and backs are shielded by rigid iron plates, laced or riveted together. Their arms and thighs are covered with chain mail or panels of tough rawhide. All this armour is hot, stiff and weighs 18 kilos! If you were a warrior, you'd have to wear it, or die!

Just don't ask me to get up.

SAMURAI ARMOUR makes running or jumping difficult, and you'd need help to take it off and put it on.

Handy hint

Stand well back! Modern guns, introduced from Europe soon after AD 1542, can shoot very far and very fast.

YOUR HELMET should be a work of art, made of 32 separate pieces. Could you afford to have one made?

YOUR ANGRY FACE-MASK should look fearsome – but it's hard to see while wearing one.

YOUR SURCOAT (cloth overcoat) must be splendid and must display your family badge on the back. But it's a tight fit over all that armour, and might make walking difficult!

Thunk!

THE CREST on top of your helmet will stick up high – beware of low-hanging objects!

Lower ranks, less protection

ASHIGARU (ordinary soldiers) wear armour made of thin, lightweight strips of metal. It's better than nothing but it's a poor defence against swords, arrows and bullets!

Metal bullets? That's not fair!

13

Could you hop onto a horse?

Traditionally, Japanese people have always fought on foot. Now, samurai ride horses. They rely on horses to charge into battle or to carry them through enemy territory. Horses are much stronger and faster than humans. But horses are expensive and often get injured. They need stables in winter, and grass or hay all year round – these are scarce in Japan, especially in mountain regions. Even worse, falls from horseback, in training as well as in battle, can be dangerous. So think carefully! If you could be a samurai, would you really be happy on a horse?

The ideal warhorse

IS NOT TOO BIG –
so you can mount and
dismount quickly.

IS VERY FAST –
to carry you out of
danger.

Handy hint

Be thankful that Japan's
old enemies – Mongol
warriors – invented
stirrups. Without
them, you could
fall off your
horse during a
battle!

Now that's what
I call a high
horse!

CAN JUMP HIGH –
to get you over
obstacles on the
battlefield.

Training on horseback

YOU'LL BE ASKED to
practise battle techniques by
racing along on horseback
while shooting arrows at a
target. Sometimes this target
is made of wood or straw, but
sometimes it's a live dog!

Yikes!

IS STRONG –
to carry you,
your armour
and all your
weapons.

IS OBEDIENT –
if not, you face
disaster!

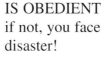

Stop right
there!

15

Could you be loyal to a lord?

Just now, Japan is at peace. But for over 400 years, from 1185 to 1590, Japan was torn apart by bloody civil wars, with fighting led by various *daimyo* (lords). Most lords were heads of noble families, but some began life as samurai. Each lord controlled a vast area of land and ruled it like a private kingdom. Lords had their own armies, made up of loyal samurai.

There are still many great, rich lords in Japan, and they still need samurai to serve them. To join a lord's army, samurai have to swear undying loyalty, and vow to obey without question. Could you ever make such powerful promises?

From samurai to warlord

MANY OF TODAY'S great families first became powerful by fighting. Starting as young samurai from poor but noble families, they won fame and riches by conquering land and capturing enemy castles. Now they rank as daimyo, and are proud and powerful.

Castles guard lords' lands and are status symbols.

Farmers pay taxes and rent by giving food to their lord.

Private armies of samurai guard lords and property.

The greatest warlord of all

SHOGUN TOKUGAWA IEYASU, who lived from 1542 to 1616, was the mightiest warlord of recent times – and perhaps the greatest ever. He defeated rival warlords in 1603 and took total control of the Japanese government. He passed strict new laws to end centuries of fighting between rival daimyo and their samurai armies.

My family, the Tokugawa, will rule Japan until 1867!

Wives from ancient noble families help lords to win political power.

Looted treasures add to lords' riches.

Poor, weak nobles are jealous.

Family crests, displayed on flags and clothes, are signs of power.

Splendid tombs are lasting memorials.

Are you strong and self-disciplined?

 re you healthy and athletic? Lean and trim? Are your muscles tough and brawny? A samurai must keep fit at all times. His body is one of his weapons! Martial arts, hard exercise and fasting will also help him to control his mind and body. So will a moderate, sober lifestyle, ritual baths and regular prayer and meditation. All of these things will purify him and prepare him to follow *Bushido*, the samurai behaviour code, also known as 'the way of the warrior'.

A true samurai must put duty first – ignoring his own hopes and fears, and sometimes the needs of his family. Do you think you could ever do this – and would you want to?

> The sword, the mind and the body are one.

The path of Zen

INNER PEACE. Zen is a way of following the Buddhist religion that has been taught in Japan since soon after the AD 1200s. It is especially popular with samurai.

Zen teachers, most of whom are monks, encourage their followers to seek enlightenment (spiritual understanding) through meditation, feats of bravery and endurance.

Bushido demands:

Swoosh!

- Honesty

- Bravery

- Skill

- Loyalty

- Self-discipline

- Obedience

Could you make the grade?

Handy hint

As a warrior, you're never off duty! Take this advice from Takeda, a wise samurai: 'Keep your sword with you at all times, even when you are alone.'

Zen gardens

STRESSED OUT? If a samurai is finding it tough to obey the Bushido code, they take some time out to meditate in a beautiful, harmonious Zen garden. The tranquil surroundings will help free their mind from fears and worries, so that they can find inner strength.

What is the sound of one hand clapping?

Courageous comrades

Even if you could become a high-ranking, well-trained samurai, you'd be just one among thousands. Before the early 1600s, when the shogun began to force lords to make peace, great daimyo kept private armies of over 100,000 men! Today these armies are smaller, but they are still formidable fighting machines.

In battle, every soldier has a vital part to play. His comrades rely on him to do his duty and be courageous. If he fails, or is cowardly, their lives might be in danger. Battles sound exciting and glorious, but that's the opinion of the survivors! War is bloody and brutal – and very, very frightening.

Swish!

Swipe!

Can't we talk about this?

AS A SAMURAI SWORDSMAN on horseback, you'd charge towards the enemy alongside troops armed with many other fighting skills: archers, spear-throwers, gunmen and foot-soldiers armed with heavy wooden sticks or long, lethal knives.

Handy hint

To display your brilliance on the battlefield, bring home some heads of slaughtered enemies!

Dangerous honour

IN BATTLE, samurai and ordinary soldiers rally round nobori (banners) bearing their warlord's badge. Being chosen to carry a banner on your back is a great honour – but very dangerous, as you become an easy target!

Would you live for weeks in the wild?

Are you a homebody? Do you like to be warm and cosy? If you were a samurai, you'd be away from home for weeks, months or even years. You'd be out on patrol, guarding your lord's land, or you'd be advancing into enemy territory. You'd sleep rough, climb mountains, face snow in winter and heavy rain in summer and go short of food. To top it off, you'd be at constant risk from enemy attack!

The 'joys' of campaign life:

HEAVY GOING.
You'd be weighed down by weapons, your sleeping mat and food rations.

JUST A SCRATCH.
Your armour – worn all the time – might get infested by lice.

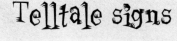

SCARY STUFF. At night, strange noises would keep you awake – are they signs of danger?

Hoot!

I want my mum!

BORING MEALS. Every day, your meals would be the same – boiled rice and (if you're lucky) dried tuna.

DESPERATE TIMES.
If you ran out of rations, you'd have to catch wild animals to survive!

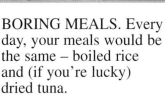

Handy hint

Did you bring a cooking pot to boil water and cook dinner? Probably not – they're heavy and fragile. Use your helmet instead!

Telltale signs

HOW DO you know if an enemy is approaching? You could send scouts to look for them – but they might be caught and killed. You could ask local people – but they might betray you. It would be safer to keep lookout for telltale signs, such as smoke from campfires or birds disturbed by the marching enemy, squawking and flapping in the distance.

Could you climb into a castle?

Defensive devices

1. Ramparts (outer defences)
2. Deep moats
3. Steep, sloping stone bases
4. High outer walls
5. Smooth, sheer walls of central keep
6. Watchtowers for lookouts
7. Small, narrow windows

For the past 100 years and more, great lords have built magnificent castles in many parts of Japan. These castles are homes for themselves and their families, barracks for their samurai soldiers, offices for the staff who manage their lands – and, of course, mighty fortresses. In 1600, Shogun Tokugawa Ieyasu seized 87 castles in the richest parts of Japan, and banished their owners to remote regions, where he hoped they could do no harm. Now, some of these lords want to send samurai to recapture their castles. This will not be easy – each building was specially designed to withstand attack.

7

6

5

Handy hint

If you can't climb into a castle, use fire! Castles' inner walls are built of wood and plaster, and burn very quickly.

Prince Yamato

ONE FAMOUS STORY tells how legendary samurai Prince Yamato (see page 11) disguised himself as an old woman to trick the samurai guarding his enemy's castle. With traditional Japanese respect for old age, the guards graciously invited 'her' to enter!

Ooh, what a helpful young man you are!

No problem, granny.

Do you love honour over life?

Just suppose you could achieve your dream, and became a samurai. Could you maintain the high standards of behaviour that everyone would expect from you? Your family, your lord, your comrades and your friends would all take pride in your fighting skills. They would share your joys and triumphs, but how would you – and they – feel if you failed?

THESE THINGS would bring shame on you and your family:

Aaah!

Running away in battle

I heard my daimyo keeps his gold in his...

Making foolish decisions that may lead to defeat in battle

Betraying your lord for money or power

One of the worst things a samurai can do is bring shame to his nearest and dearest. If samurai murder, cheat, lie, steal, betray comrades or let themselves get captured, they might be tempted to choose death rather than dishonour. But listen carefully – harming yourself is never, ever the right thing to do! Always remember that it's much better to stay alive and learn from your failures. Just try not to make the same mistakes again.

Being responsible for a comrade's death

Handy hint

Try to lead a good, honest life! That way, you'll be remembered, and honoured with an ornate tomb when you die.

Stealing, lying, cheating or committing some other crime

Getting captured by enemies

Try to stay alive!

JAPANESE DOCTORS do their best to heal injured samurai. But if there's no doctor nearby, try kanpo (traditional remedies), such as bathing wounds with heated urine, or eating horse-dung mixed with water to stop bleeding!

Whose idea was this?

The myth of Minamoto no Tametomo

SAMURAI Minamoto no Tametomo was said to have killed himself rather than face defeat. But he was also said to have won 20 battles in just two years, and to have one arm that was magically longer than the other! Are any of these stories really true?

The last samurai?

You'll find this hard to believe, but several hundred years from now, there will be no more samurai in Japan. If you could travel into the future, you'd find that laws passed by the Tokugawa family – the shoguns who rule Japan – mean that samurai warriors are no longer needed.

There will be peace at home in Japan, and very little contact with foreigners. Samurai will keep their rank and their traditions, but will no longer be warriors. In 1867, there will be a revolution, and the last Tokugawa shogun will be overthrown. New Japanese industries will develop – and samurai will be history!

The future lies with industry and business, not old-fashioned samurai.

But the samurai way should not be forgotten.

...though their fame will live forever!

IN THEIR DREAMS, kids today can still join a samurai army and share in their glorious adventures. Millions of children around the world are fascinated by samurai.

Handy hint

Study martial arts and take part in a living tradition. Kendo, judo and karate are all based on samurai skills.

HONOURABLE MEMORY. Samurai bravery, loyalty and noble self-sacrifice will inspire soldiers, sailors and airmen for centuries.

PROUD HERITAGE. Some samurai castles will be carefully preserved, so that everyone can marvel at their strength and beauty.

ON DISPLAY. Samurai weapons and armour will be put on show in museums, for visitors to study and admire.

MEDIA HEROES. Samurai warriors will star in epic adventures in films, computer games and manga cartoon books.

Glossary

Ashigaru An ordinary soldier in a Japanese warlord's army, lower-ranking than samurai.

Buddhist Someone who follows the teachings of the spiritual leader known as the Buddha (the Enlightened One), who lived on the Indian Subcontinent around 550 BC. The Buddha taught his followers to live thoughtful, honest, peaceful lives to try to help end suffering.

Bushido Rules for good behaviour that samurai were meant to follow. Also known as 'the way of the warrior'.

Chain mail Flexible armour made by joining hundreds of small metal rings together.

Daimyo A lord who owned large estates and was the head of a noble family. Often, a daimyo also led his own samurai army.

Enlightenment Spiritual truth and understanding.

Genbuku A ceremony at the end of samurai training to mark the time when a teenage boy became a man and a warrior.

Go An ancient board game. As in chess, winning is based on intelligence and strategy (careful planning).

Kanpo Traditional Japanese medicine.

Katana A long, curved sword, worn with the sharp edge of the blade uppermost.

Manga Brightly illustrated comic books that sometimes feature samurai heroes. They are very popular in modern Japan.

Martial arts Combat sports based on warriors' fighting techniques. They include judo (unarmed contests using balance and self-control), karate (contests using the hands) and kendo (contests using swords).

Meditation A spiritual practice which involves sitting quietly for a long period of time.

Moderate Mild and calm – not excessive.

Mongols An east Asian people famous for their fighting skills. They ruled an empire stretching from China to the Black Sea in the 1200s.

Nobori Banners carried by warriors, usually decorated with the badge of their lord or battle-commander.

Ramparts The defensive walls of a castle.

Rawhide The tough, untreated skin of an animal.

Samurai ('men who serve') Expert warriors who fought in armies led by great Japanese lords between about AD 1200 and 1600.

Shogun The most senior soldier in Japan, who led national armies on behalf of the emperor. The title means 'great general'. From 1185 to 1867, shoguns were the effective rulers of Japan.

Surcoat A tunic or cloak, made of cloth, sometimes worn to cover samurai armour. Often decorated with a lord's or battle-commander's badge.

Tsuba A circular or oval guard fitted next to the handle of a sword to protect the fingers from the sharp blade.

Zen A way of following the Buddhist faith that was popular among samurai soldiers. It encourages meditation, self-discipline and endurance.

Index